The Tyneham Story

by Robert Westwood

with contributions by Lynda Price

Inspiring Places Publishing
2 Down Lodge Close
Alderholt
Fordingbridge
Hants
SP6 3JA
ISBN 978-0-9928073-1-3

Contains Ordnance Survey data © Crown copyright and database right (2011)

Inspiring places

Contents

Guide for Visitors

There is a large car park, entrance to Tyneham is free but a donation towards the upkeep of the village is requested. There is no café, shop or drinking water available. There are toilets near the farm, including ones for the disabled. Picnic tables are provided - please take all your litter home. Dogs are welcome but should be kept under close control. If you choose to pick up after your dog, please be prepared to take it home.

You are free to wander around the village but please do not cross barriers and enter restricted areas. You must keep to paths between yellow markers.

Opening Times

Tyneham is open most weekends and during school holidays. For a recorded message of opening times please phone 01929 404819. Further information can be found at www.tynehamopc.org.uk, the online parish clerks website run by volunteers.

How to get there

On the A351 from Wareham to Corfe Castle, take the small road signed Kimmeridge. At the top of Ridgeway Hill turn right through gateway (shut when ranges are closed). The road to Tyneham is a little way along on the left. Alternatively approach from East Lulworth.

Grid Reference SY 882803

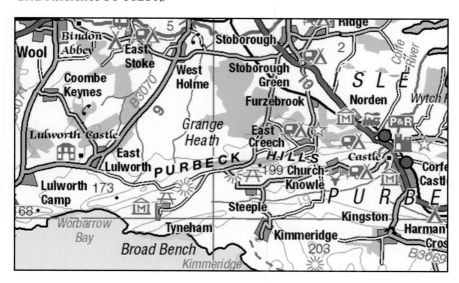

4

Extract from:
Intimations of Immortality
There was a time when meadow, grove, and stream,
The earth, and every common sight,
To me did seem
Apparelled in celestial light,
The glory and the freshness of a dream.
It is not now as it hath been of yore;—
Turn wheresoe'er I may,
By night or day,
The things which I have seen I now can see no more.

William Wordsworth

Tyneham is a small, deserted village in the south-west corner of Purbeck. It has not been inhabited since December 1943 when it was requisitioned by the army for use in training for the D-Day landings. It has been part of the Lulworth Firing Range ever since, a facility where all sections of the army are trained in the use of armoured fighting vehicles. Before the war Tyneham was a secluded agricultural community, part of the estate of the Bond family who lived in a magnificent Elizabethan manor house. It had a pretty church, a schoolhouse and post office. Today it is one of the area's most popular tourist attractions with visitors drawn by its history, tranquility and natural beauty. However, it is used by the military during the week but open to the public most weekends and during the school holidays; it is still part of a live firing range. There is nothing to spend your money on here apart from a requested donation for car parking. It is a fascinating reminder of a lost, rural way of life.

The road to Tyneham- 2014
One hundred years after the photograph on the back cover was taken - man has moved on but the beautiful view remains. St Mary's Church is still nestling between the trees with the land climbing to Flower's Barrow beyond. The steep chalk slope of Bindon Hill can be seen in the mid distance with Mupe Rocks scattered in the sea to the left. The long arm of Portland lies on the horizon with the distinctive cone shape of Worbarrow Tout in the picture below.

Introduction

With its quaint stone villages, rugged coastline, ancient ruins and its traditional Victorian seaside resort of Swanage, Purbeck seems to embody much that is treasured in the English countryside. Rich agricultural land nestles between two ridges, one of chalk and the other limestone, that run east to west from the margins of Swanage Bay. A few small villages and many farmsteads have long cultivated the soft sands and clays of the valley between the twin ridges, while nearer the coast the settlements have concentrated on quarrying the Portland and Purbeck limestones. Much of this productive land was once owned and managed by a number of small but prosperous estates centred around fine manors, three of them the property of the Bond family. Some, such as Encombe and Smedmore, are still thriving, their land well tended by tenant farmers and their splendid houses well maintained by wealthy owners. However, it is a small estate at the western end of Purbeck, its manor long gone and its houses lying derelict, that now attracts most interest.

Few villages can have had a more idyllic setting than Tyneham. At this part of Purbeck the chalk and limestone ridges are closer together and the narrowed vale that separates them feels more intimate and homely. The ridges and the valley end at Worbarrow, a delightful bay, sculpted out of the softer sediments between the harder rocks, that once provided a sheltered haven for fishermen and smugglers. The village sits a short distance inland and now lies in ruins, although the school and church are still intact and the roofless cottages have been made safe.

The story of Tyneham has a powerful appeal and many are aware of the bare facts: a village taken over by the army just before Christmas 1943 to be used as a practice area for the D-Day landings, its inhabitants removed from their homes forever (despite apparent promises to the contrary); a sacrifice willingly made for the common good. At the time, due to the need for secrecy, this event passed largely unnoticed by those not directly involved, but from our modern perspective it seems particularly poignant. This was a village quintessentially English; picturesque and geographically isolated, tiny cottages clustered around a village green, a church, small school and imposing vicarage. Most depended for a living on the great house or the fishing from the charming bay nearby, to which, in the heat of summer, the children would wander down after school. The peace of this rural idyll was shattered, not by enemy bombs, but by the need for allied troops to train for the forthcoming invasion. Today it is a fitting reminder that sacrifices were made by all levels of society.

History

Ancient and medieval

Purbeck is an ancient landscape, the heathland north of Povington Hill is littered with Bronze Age burial barrows, and on the very edge of the Chalk cliffs above Worbarrow Bay sits the Iron Age hillfort of Flower's Barrow, one of many forcibly taken by the Romans in 43AD. Almost half of it has disappeared, providing geologists with a useful means of quantifying the rate of erosion here.

In the Domesday Book, compiled towards the end of the eleventh century, there are four Tynehams mentioned (then called Tigeham), representing the present village and the neighbouring settlements of North and South Egliston and Baltington; this was a well developed Saxon landscape before the Norman invasion. The Tyneham which includes the present village was held by Bretel St. Clair on behalf of Robert, Count of Mortain and half-brother to William the Conqueror. Robert was one of England's major landowners at the time, having been well rewarded for his support in the conquest. The history of the manor in medieval times is unclear but from the early thirteenth century it was in the hands of a family called Russell who held it for six generations. This era saw a tremendous

Looking down on Worbarrow Bay from Flower's Barrow.

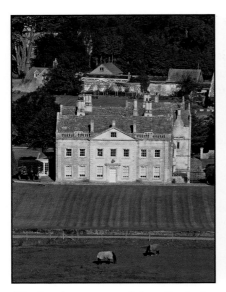

The Bonds once owned three Purbeck estates. On the left is Creech Grange, bought by Nathaniel Bond in 1686. It remained in the hands of the Bond family until 1979. On the right is Holme Priory, acquired by the Bonds in 1690 and still home to a branch of the family.

growth of the population across England prompted by relative peace and a warm climate. Purbeck was already well cultivated and farmers made use of any land they could. Even the steep sides of Tyneham Cap south-east of the village were ploughed and strip lynchets, the remains of terraces on hillsides, are common in the area.

The Bond family arrives at Tyneham

In 1563 the estate was bought by John Williams for his son Henry and by 1583 Tyneham House was complete. In 1683 it was bought by Nathaniel Bond, an Oxford educated barrister who became MP for Corfe Castle in 1689. He also bought the neighbouring estate of Creech Grange in 1686. This magnificent house can be seen from the road towards Wareham. In 1690 the Bonds also purchased Holme Priory, a lovely house dating from the sixteenth century near Wareham. For well over two centuries the Bonds occupied these three Purbeck estates and one, Holme Priory, is still the home of a Bond family.

The Tyneham estate was managed by seven generations of the Bond family until the forced evacuation in 1943. Many family members were prominent locally and nationally, a number serving with distinction in the army.

Life in the Early Twentieth Century

Many of Dorset's villages have a long history; Saxon names are common, indicating habitation for a thousand years or more. Scattered ancient churches and medieval field patterns remind us that this county has long been a land of small settlements dependent on agriculture. Today village life is very different, even the smallest hamlets now have the latest modern conveniences and the natural beauty and tranquility of the landscape, coupled with modern transport, has led to villages being home to city workers and to being a second, holiday home for many. Dorset's great literary genius Thomas Hardy has famously captured the harsh realities of nineteenth century rural life in tragic novels such as *Tess of the D'Urbervilles*. However, by the turn of the twentieth century life in the country had been made somewhat easier by developments in agricultural machinery and as the century progressed improvements in transport and infrastructure continued to benefit rural communities. Maybe if there ever was a rural idyll it would have been in a quiet, secluded village nestling in a picturesque, sheltered valley where fertile land and a benevolent squire ensured all of an industrious nature would live well and happily?

Post Office Row in 1929. The long building on the left is Laundry Cottages.

Part of the fascination of Tyneham is that the village, although in ruins, is as it was left in 1943 and prompts us to imagine what life was like in an isolated rural community in the first half of the twentieth century. It is easy to picture Tyneham as a rural idyll but there is no doubt that life was very hard and luxuries were scarce. Nevertheless, there is enough evidence and accounts from those who lived here during those times to suggest that this was a happy community who depended on each other for almost every aspect of their lives.

The 1911 census reveals fifty nine men of working age in Tyneham. Of these around thirty were farmers, farm labourers, cattlemen or shepherds. There were seven fishermen who made their living at Worbarrow Bay and a few men who were general labourers. There was a schoolmaster, a carter, an estate woodman, an odd job man, a postmaster, a footman and, of course, a vicar. As might be expected from the time, many of the women were not listed as having an occupation – men were invariably described as the "head" of the household and their spouse simply as "wife". Those that were listed as having an occupation were servants, maids or laundry workers. There was also a certified midwife. The previous census in 1901 listed seven men

There were several farms in and around the village owned by Tyneham and neighbouring Bond estates. Helen Taylor recalls the village street filled with sound on Thursdays as sheep, pigs and calves were taken to market.

Above: Shearing sheep in 1917.
Left: Haymaking in 1929. Horses were still important for such tasks despite the fact that Henry Ford had mass produced tractors since 1917.

Tyneham at the turn of last century. Note the telegraph pole, the Post Office had the only telephone until 1935, only used for incoming and outgoing telegrams.

employed by the Coastguard Station and the closure of this in 1912 had a major impact on the village, especially the school population.

To help us picture life in this pretty and self-sufficient village we have accounts from former residents. *Tyneham – A Lost Heritage* was written by Lilian Bond, the daughter of William Henry Bond who had inherited Tyneham in 1898. Lilian was born in 1887 and lived in the village from 1898 until 1914 when she was married in Tyneham Church. She writes of a "golden age" of evenings walking in the woods, of picnics and bathing at Worbarrow Bay and of friendships and community spirit fostered by their secluded, beautiful surroundings. Her love, and knowledge, of nature seems an inevitable consequence of her environment.

Helen Taylor, a seamstress at Tyneham House who lived in the village up until the evacuation in 1943 has also shared many reminiscences, some of which are recounted in *Tyneham - the lost village of Dorset* by Andrew Norman and Mary Hurst. Although of a much lower social standing than Lilian, Helen too looks back with fond memories of life in Tyneham. Working hard was not optional and old age could bring multiple difficulties, but it is clear from her accounts that the Bond family looked after "their" villagers and presided over a happy and caring community.

Tyneham House in the 1850s. This fine Elizabethan house was completed in 1583.

Tyneham School class of 1927. The school was established by the Reverend Nathaniel Bond in 1860 and closed in 1932 when only nine children remained on the register.

George Richards with his sister Mrs. Manktelow.
A farm labourer all his life, Helen Taylor
remembers him as the last adult to wear a smock.

The Post Office in 1943, the year of the evacuation; by now
motor vehicles were more common. Rex stands guard!

Worbarrow

The Coastguard Service was officially founded in 1822, combining a number of roles that had initially been set up to combat the widespread smuggling trade that flourished in the eighteenth and early nineteenth centuries. Worbarrow Bay was a popular drop-off point for smugglers and there are many tales of the smugglers' activities around this area. Brandy Bay beneath Gad Cliff perhaps tells its own story. At the beginning of the twentieth century smuggling had ceased to be such a major problem and the work of the Coastguard Service had diversified. Keeping watch for shipping, signalling, looking after wrecks and lifesaving were parts of its many duties. In the census of 1901 over fifty people were recorded as residing in this tiny coastal hamlet, over half of them from the families of the seven Coastguard men, living in the Coastguard Cottages on the edge of the bay. Helen Taylor recounts that the fishermen and the Coastguards did not always get on well. The fishermen found the wood from shipwrecks very useful, but salvage was the responsibility of the Coastguard Service. She also suggests that smuggling may have still been prevalent in her time, and recalls seeing a man she guessed was a Customs officer on horseback

A picnic in front of the Coastguard Station in 1900. The station closed in 1912 and the buildings were soon demolished on the instructions of William Bond who didn't want them converted for other use. The removal of the Coastguards was keenly felt by Tyneham's school which suddenly lost nearly half its pupils.

Left: Jack, Tom and Charlie Miller. Charlie died of influenza, aged ninety-one, just a few days after the evacuation. The move, in bitter December weather, cannot have helped.

Right: Hauling in the mackerel catch. Everyone rushed to help when a shoal was sighted and dealers from Wareham were soon on the scene to box up the catch and take it to market.

one day at Worbarrow and how, when he had gone, an old woman rose to reveal two wooden kegs that she had been hiding beneath her long skirt!

The Miller family provided the bulk of Worbarrow's fishermen. Lilian Bond remembered them as a good looking family whose intimate knowledge of the sea "was an inherited lore, slowly acquired and tested, often through bitter experience." Millers had been fishing here for well over two hundred years; legend has it that they were all descended from two brothers from Scotland who had been Spanish privateers at the time of the Armada. A variety of fish were caught but it was lobsters that were the main source of income; carts daily took lobsters and a few crabs to market in Wareham. In summer there was always someone on the lookout for shoals of mackerel which might appear in the bay at any time. This caused great excitement as everyone rushed to help capture and haul in the shoal. Several thousand at a time could be caught and a telegram from the Coastguard Station quickly brought dealers and their carts from Wareham. The fish were hurriedly boxed up and taken to market but enough remained for the villagers to feast on.

Above is Worbarrow Bay as it is today with the ruins of Sea Cottage in the foreground. Right is Sea Cottage, as it was, home to Henry Miller's son Jack and his wife Alice White Rose. They were evacuated in 1943, both aged 77. Below is "Sheepleaze" a large "second home" built by London barrister Warwick Draper in 1910 with the permission of William Bond. Nothing now remains of this.

The Army Arrives

1916 was an inglorious year in the history of the British Army. The carnage on the Somme had made it apparent that new tactics and equipment would be needed to break the deadlock of trench warfare. Armoured vehicles that could cross all terrain would be part of the response - the tank was born. Little did the villagers of Tyneham know, that this would eventually lead to them being driven from their homes.

Many communities across the country were shattered by the terrible events of 1914-1918 and Tyneham suffered its own losses. The memorial plaque in St. Mary's Church, Tyneham lists six men of the village who lost their lives in the conflict, including Helen Taylor's brother Bertie, killed in action at Gallipoli in 1916 and her step-brother William Meech who was killed in Egypt. She also lost her other brother Arthur in Palestine. Helen's mother died, aged fifty two, in 1917, worn out, she says in Andrew Norman's and Mary Hurst's book, with worry, work and grief.

It was another, more local event in 1916, that was to have far reaching consequences for the village. In October that year the newly formed Tank Corps took over Bovington Camp which had been acquired by the army in 1899 as an infantry training area. A great deal of secrecy accompanied this event with farmers and villagers being told to stay indoors and not to look as strange machines trundled through sleepy Dorset lanes. The eventual success of the tank ensured that, after the war, the Corps became a priority for expansion, despite the advocacy of some of the "old guard" who believed the horse was still the answer to mobile warfare. After much protest from local landowners the gunnery school at Lulworth was formed and by the time the Second World War began the people of Purbeck had long been used to a considerable military presence.

1918. A tank has come to grief on Wool bridge. Terrible jams and delays were common on the roads as the tanks made their way from Bovington to practice on the Bindon Hill Range at Lulworth.

Evacuation

The firing ranges near Lulworth at Bindon Hill were extended in 1938 and the RAF soon developed a radar installation above Brandy Bay, south of Tyneham, surrounded by anti-aircraft gun emplacements. RAF personnel were billeted in the village where the army had already taken over some empty cottages. Tyneham had been in decline for some time: the Coastguard had departed in the early part of the century and a number of farm labourers had left as their work became more mechanised. When around sixty of the Women's Auxiliary Air Force came to man the radar station they were placed in Tyneham House and Ralph Bond, who had inherited the estate from his father William in 1935, soon found him and his family displaced and living in Gardener's Cottage. Ralph enthusiastically organised and led Tyneham's Home Guard platoon and his son Mark joined the Rifle Brigade and was soon commissioned.

By 1943 Tyneham's dwindling population had already made sacrifices and accepted changes to their way of life for the sake of the war effort: they were well used to a military presence. Most, if not all, would have believed, however, that their peaceful pre-war existence would resume once the war was over. Ralph Bond certainly assumed that his ancestral home would be returned to him and that he would be able, once more, to pursue his love of the natural world.

Training for D-Day

It was becoming increasingly clear to the Allies' military planners that training for the invasion of mainland Europe would require extensive facilities, including suitable stretches of coast. Thus it was that, towards the end of 1943, the War Cabinet decided to evacuate the whole of the Tyneham valley so that it could be used as an army training ground. On the 16th November 1943 letters were posted to the 225 inhabitants in 102 properties, informing them that they had to leave their homes by 19th December. The letter informed them that this was necessary to give troops the required space to train using the latest equipment and to practise with live ammunition. It is worth remembering that the army faced major problems in training thousands of new recruits without previous battle experience and that Tyneham was not the only village to be requisitioned in this way. Imber in Wiltshire and Stanford in Norfolk were similarly appropriated. The population of Purbeck was swelled by thousands of allied soldiers and it was mainly American tank crew that trained in the Tyneham area; many of them took part in the fateful landings at Omaha Beach.

The villagers move out

The villagers were told that everything possible would be done to provide compensation and to help them find other accommodation. The letter closed by saying, "The government realise that this is no small sacrifice which you are asked to make, but they are sure you will give this further help towards winning the war with a good heart." They were also told that when the War Department had no further use for the land they would have every right to return to their homes. An office was set up in Wareham to provide help and advice for those who needed it, and the whole process was conducted in great secrecy.

1943 was a particularly harsh winter and the experience of packing up and moving was both harrowing and heartbreaking for many. Farmers sold their livestock and farm implements and the Bonds hurriedly stored precious belongings in the cellar of the great house, unable to organise the removal of everything in the short time. Evelyn Bond, wife of Ralph, helped a local council official find vacant properties for the villagers. As Helen Taylor wrote: "People's lives, in fact a whole way of life, disintegrated in a short space of time." A community had ceased to exist and its inhabitants, some old and frail, were no longer able to offer each other the mutual support that had been such a feature of village life. At a time of personal

In Memory of Elizabeth Daughter of James and Martha Mellor who Departed this Life

and national crisis, this must have been a cruel blow; but the villagers were aware that they needed to make another sacrifice for the war effort and were resigned to their fate. Evelyn Bond was the last to leave; famously, she pinned a note to the door of the church before she left. It read:

"Please treat the church and houses with care. We have given up our homes where many of us have lived for generations, to help win the war to keep men free. We shall return one day and thank you for treating the village kindly."

A reconstruction of Evelyn Bond pinning the note on the church door.

The villagers were largely tenants of the Bonds and the only compensation they received was quite literally the value of the vegetables in their gardens. Farmers were forced to sell livestock and farm implements, often at artificially low prices as buyers were aware of their need to sell. Vacant properties in the surrounding area were taken over to house the evacuees and many of the farm labourers found work on other farms. The Bonds

found a house in Corfe Castle, as did Helen Taylor's family. A number of older villagers found adjusting to their new situation extremely difficult and some, such as Charlie Miller, died soon afterwards. Some found indoor sanitation and electric lights a real blessing but most mourned the loss of their homes and the fellowship of their neighbours.

Above: Shepherd Bill Upshall, evacuated in 1943. Right: Ration books of the Everett family of Tyneham.

Left: Ernest Whitelock (centre) at Tyneham Farm, 1942. Tractors had only recently been introduced at Tyneham. Ernest was evacuated with his wife Evelyn.

After the War

Before the war had ended suspicions were beginning to form that the War Office intended to keep hold of the land it had seized. Early in 1945 members of the Wareham and Purbeck Rural District Council, including Ralph Bond who had been elected member for Tyneham, were expressing their concern that the purely emergency appropriation of land might lead to people permanently losing their homes and that members of the public might lose access to areas of outstanding natural beauty. By May 1945, when the war in Europe had ended, permanent road barriers had been constructed at Steeple and there was still much army activity in the Tyneham valley. The council sent a deputation to Whitehall and were politely listened to, although it was pointed out that national interests would come first. In fact the army did give up much of the land they had requisitioned in Purbeck, but Tyneham was not included; it continued to be a part of the firing ranges.

A public enquiry

In February 1947, Prime Minister Clement Atlee told Parliament that it had not been possible to reconcile military needs with the interests of the local people as far as Purbeck was concerned, but promised a public enquiry before any permanent decision was made. This took place in March 1948 in Wareham. The case for the residents was led by Lord Hinchingbrooke, the local Conservative MP. He made much of the the

pledge made by the war time government and revealed how he had visited the site of the evacuation in November 1943 and reassured the departing villagers that their homes would be there for them when the war was over.

By 1949 there were numerous warning notices along the road between Lulworth Camp and East Lulworth and the beautiful Tyneham valley was becoming more and more wild and overgrown.

Ralph Bond and the last vicar of Tyneham, Reverend H. C. Money, also spoke out for the return of the land. For their case the army admitted that pledges had been made to the villagers of Tyneham at the time of evacuation but argued that new, unforeseen circumstances dictated that the army should now retain the land. In particular, although it wasn't explicitly stated, the emerging Cold War meant that Britain's armed forces should continue to train for future conflicts. Bigger tanks and bigger armaments also demanded more space and the fact that the ranges were next to the sea was clearly convenient. The enquiry's report was considered by the Ministry for Town and Country Planning who decided that national interest should come first and that the army could compulsorily purchase the land. There were conditions, and the government was encouraged to compensate the evacuees generously. It was agreed that this meant not only those who owned land but also those who had been tenants and the government funded the council to enable them to build homes for the villagers which they could rent at roughly what they were paying previously. In some cases they bought the houses that the villagers were already in but they also built a new council estate in Sandford near Wareham, renaming the road "Tyneham Close". Many were now comfortably placed and enjoying electricity and indoor sanitation.

Tyneham House in the 1950s. The house quickly deteriorated, thieves stole lead from the roof and water began to do immense damage inside. In the late 1960s the army began giving away historic parts of the house to other Dorset houses.

Post Office Row, Tyneham in the 1960s.

The loss of a rural idyll

In 1956 Lilian Bond, sister of Ralph, published her *Tyneham – A Lost Heritage*. The foreword was written by the distinguished historian Sir Arthur Bryant who eulogised about the beauty and heritage of Purbeck, calling it "a kind of inner shrine of coastal England". A few years before he had leased neighbouring Smedmore House and on St George's Day 1949 had written an article for the Illustrated London News lamenting the loss of a romantic, idyllic England. Tyneham was his inspiration for this and he claimed to have wandered, accidentally, onto the army ranges, finding the decaying, overgrown village and the sad, boarded up remains of Tyneham House. In the next few years others continued to express their sorrow for the loss of what they imagined had been a rural utopia and their anger over the betrayal of its honest, industrious inhabitants.

Their dismay increased in December 1959 when the Ministry of Transport published proposals to close permanently around forty public footpaths on the ranges. In January 1961 another public enquiry was held, this time in Dorchester, and despite powerful objections from the Purbeck District Council and eminent locals, including Colonel Joseph Weld from Lulworth, the enquiry gave permission for the army to close the footpaths providing it granted public access to Tyneham and Worbarrow Bay during public holidays.

The Tyneham Action Group

Then, in 1968, the cause was taken up by a young Dorset reporter named Rodney Legg who had recently started Dorset; The County Magazine. Encouraged by others, including the well-known writer Monica Hutchings, he formed the Tyneham Action Group. As the name implies,

Legg anticipated that the group would do more than merely petition for the retreat of the army from parts of Purbeck, and would march, protest and engage in activities just within the law. Legg originally suggested that the land be given to the National Trust who, he envisaged, would protect and nurture the landscape while making it, once more, accessible to the public. At the inaugural meeting he set out his ideas, but was followed by others who had different aims. In particular Rolf Gardiner, a rural revivalist, argued that the Tyneham valley should be returned to its previous owners. This view prevailed and it became the expressed aim of the group. The chairmanship of the group was trusted to Philip Draper, the son of Warwick Draper who had built a second home, Sheepleaze, at Worbarrow and vice presidents included Lilian Bond and the Tory peer, Lord Salisbury who had previously been MP for South Dorset.

The group's first major action was a widely publicised mass gathering at Tyneham on August Bank Holiday 1968. The roads were jammed and the group was encouraged by the strength of public interest. Mark Bond, son of Ralph, was supportive of the group's aims but, as a brigadier in the army, had to be careful about his involvement. After a while differences within the group began to emerge and Rodney Legg eventually left and formed another action group, the 1943 Committee. Legg was strongly opposed to what he saw as an attempt to hand Tyneham back to rich landowners whose aims for the land would be centred around profit. He wanted Tyneham to be in the care of the National Trust, to be a sanctuary for wildlife and a place of beauty for all to enjoy. He was not afraid to use more radical methods than the original Action Group, indulging in minor vandalism and disrupting meetings.

The Nugent Report

The hopes and dreams of the activists seemed to have been realised in July 1973 when Lord Nugent's Defence Lands Committee published its report recommending the removal of the Lulworth Gunnery School to a site in Wales. Tyneham was to be released, but to whom? It soon became clear that the land would be offered to the original landowners to buy back. This was an unattractive option for most; it would require a great deal of money to restore the land to its original purpose. Rodney Legg's dream of some kind of national park was looking less and less likely. It was also becoming clear that many local people, particularly the inhabitants of Lulworth, did not want the Army to leave. The military contributed significantly to the local economy and there was a growing feeling that the Army was protecting the land from modern development. Then, in 1974, a government white paper rejected the Nugent report and declared that the Gunnery School would stay in Lulworth and that Tyneham would remain part of the firing ranges. The Tyneham Action Group reluctantly called an end to their operations, although Rodney Legg's band, now the Friends of Tyneham, continued their protests and appeals. There was jubilation in Lulworth and the government promised more would be done to allow public access. The Friends of Tyneham were undoubtedly uncharitable in their assessment of what Mark Bond would have done had he managed Tyneham's land, given his love and knowledge of natural history, but many would probably agree that now the Tyneham valley remains a beautiful and unspoilt corner of England's countryside.

Improved public access

In February 1975 the Army duly unveiled proposals to improve public access to the ranges and in 1978, working with local councils, created strict byelaws and began to develop public access to the village, making the buildings safe and providing information for visitors. A warden service was established and today a team of wardens maintains the access and since 1979 Tyneham has been open to the public most weekends and during school holidays.

At the end of his long and immaculately researched book about Tyneham's story, *The Village That Died For England,* Patrick Wright details the views of Helen Taylor, one of the last to leave Tyneham in 1943. She was dismissive of the action groups and admitted that, after 1948, she had no wish to return. She claimed that none of the old villagers she knew would have wanted to either, most being comfortable in their new homes. She did cherish the memory of the Tyneham she knew but was glad the Army was now the guardian of its special landscape.

Former residents and guests outside the church in 2003, sixty years after they were were evacuated. Mark Bond is second from right and Range Liaison Officer, Major Mick Burgess, is far left.

Post Office Row, or simply "The Row" is the main group of cottages in the village. With the church and pond to either side, their image must reside in many people's minds as a symbol of Tyneham. The roofs have been removed and the walls made safe so we are now free to explore these small, humble dwellings. Inside are plaques telling us who lived there and a little about what they did. They make fascinating reading.

The Post Office was the cottage with the telephone kiosk in front. The telephone kiosk only arrived in 1929; previously the village's only telephone was in the kitchen of the Post Office and was for telegrams only. The cottage next to the school was for the teacher, while the small cottage next to the Post Office "went with" the farm and housed successive labourers and farm workers. The lowest cottage in the row was traditionally occupied by the shepherd.

The Church

Lynda Price, 2014

The Church of St. Mary the Virgin stands on high ground overlooking the village street. There has been a place of worship on this site since the fourteenth century.

Today's building bears little resemblance to the tiny chapel that stood here in medieval times. Over the centuries, as the population of the valley increased, the owners of the manor of Tyneham added to, and improved, their church. It was at the heart of the village, its Rector involved in every aspect of village life, a man of money and influence, but this would count for nothing when world events swept into this quiet Dorset valley. Another chapter in the long story of this church began as the last villager left on a cold December afternoon in 1943. The south coast was to become an armed camp in preparation for D-Day. The old building was now vulnerable, measures had to be taken to protect it. The heavy oak pulpit and pews were removed, stained glass carefully transported to a place of safety and windows boarded. For over thirty years the ancient stone memorials would lie in darkness. When the village was

1975 light floods into the church after thirty years of darkness.

The memorial window to Grace Draper. Her family had a holiday home built at Worbarrow.

opened up to the public in the late 1970s coils of barbed wire guarding the approach to its heavy wooden door were removed. Builders moved in and work began to restore the church. Another chapter began.

Over seventy years have passed since a congregation worshipped in the Church of St. Mary the Virgin. The war changed this corner of Dorset for ever, but if Tyneham villagers attended their church today much would seem familiar. The oak roof of the Bond's South Transept still curves grandly over gleaming pews, the morning sun casts coloured patterns over the altar cloth as it shines through the beautiful east window and, immune from the drama of change, the medieval stone sink lies in the North Transept. Sharing the walls with the carved stone memorials to distinguished members of the Bond family is a modern addition. Photos displayed on oak boards record village life before the evacuation. A fitting memorial to a lost way of life and the sacrifice made by the ordinary people of this valley.

Tyneham Church today. The MoD are responsible for the buildings maintenance, and the day to day running of what has become a popular visitor attraction. The church has been deconsecrated and is still owned by the Diocese of Salisbury.

The School

Lynda Price, 2014

Tucked under the trees at the heart of the village, opposite the church, lies Tyneham School. Visitors can step inside the recreated schoolroom. Many remember long bench desks with inkwells from their schooldays. On the teacher's desk a cane rests beside her log book, a scrupulous daily record of the lives of her pupils during the spring of 1927. Visits from the Rector and the school nurse, saluting the flag on Empire Day followed by the excitement of an afternoon of singing and celebration. Over sixty children were taught in this school room during the early years of the last century

1976 Undisturbed since World War II, nature has quietly taken over the school.

but by the twenties the log book showed less than thirty. In bad weather the long walk to school across muddy fields kept all but a handful of village children away. The population of the valley was shrinking. The school closed for good in 1932 with only 9 pupils on the register.

The children who attended this school lived in an age before cars, electricity and digital

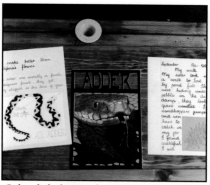

School desks, Archie Everett has a close encounter with a snake at Worbarrow

...and Vera Wellman catches Great Green Bush-crickets on Gold Down.

entertainment. Their free time was spent outside, absorbing the rich variety of wildlife in Tyneham's meadows and woods, turning stones along the Worbarrow shoreline to discover the weird creatures lurking beneath. This curiosity led to a greater knowledge of the natural world than we find in children today. When you visit the school you can share the children's discoveries. Nature Study Books are displayed on the desks for you to read. Their adventures recalled in a child's 'best joined up writing' with colourful drawings to help describe the plants and creatures they encountered. Visiting Tyneham School may bring back lost childhood memories but the flowers, birds and insects carefully illustrated and described in the nature books may be seen as you walk around the Tyneham valley today.

Life was tough in Tyneham in the early 1900s. It was hard for poorer families to send their children to school, they were needed to help at home or in the fields.

Other Cottages

Rectory Cottages lie near the school and originally formed the rectory before Nathaniel Bond, who built the school, commissioned a new rectory. A little way behind these cottages sit **Laundry Cottages**, the home of the Taylor family and so called because they did the laundry for the Bond family and rectory. Lilian Bond remembers them as having the most pleasant location in the village, sheltered and south facing. You can still see, in the back of one of the cottages, the large pit where the copper pot once stood for doing the laundry, with an open fire beneath it. Opposite Post Office Row and by the road out of the village stand the **Double Cottages**; these

Above: Laundry Cottages, home of the Taylor family.

Right: There were few modern conveniences in Tyneham. Far right is the tub where Emily Taylor did the laundry for the Bonds and the rectory. It was the only cottage with running water, others used the village tap, right.

were small and not very convenient. One was occupied for many years by George Richards who is pictured on page 13. Sitting just behind the Double Cottage is **Gardener's Cottage**, traditionally the home of the head gardener to the Bond family.

The phone box (right) is a replica but boasts authentic fittings and looks much as the original did when the village was evacuated in 1943. Tyneham's first phone box arrived in 1929; before that villagers used the phone in the Post Office. It was left to decay after the evacuation but was restored in 1983. Unfortunately this was accidentally destroyed in 1985 during the making of the film "Comrades" when Tyneham was used as a set for Tolpuddle. The film company bought a replacement which was completely refurbished in 2012. The full story is on the side of the box.

The Rectory was built by Nathaniel Bond in the mid-nineteenth century. It was delightfully situated just west of the church and separated from it by formal gardens. Although a spacious and imposing dwelling there were numerous problems caused by the pitch of the roof being too flat. Much money was spent on repairs to stop leaks.

The Rectory is now a single storey shell, but visitors can get a good idea of the grand dwelling it once was. It occupied the sunniest site in the village but was susceptible to storms and gales coming from the sea.

The Farm

Lynda Price, 2014

Work in progress, with the stables and granary behind, members of the public join the Dry Stone Walling Association on a training course at Tyneham Farm.

The long tiled roof of Tyneham Farms granary and stable is visible amongst the trees to the south of the car park. Until recently the farmstead fell within the Firing Range danger zone, out of bounds to the public. Keen to increase public access, the Army launched its Tyneham Farm Project in 2007. The farm complex opened as 'a work in progress' the following spring. Watching the volunteers work proved a great attraction in the project's early days.

Visitors could admire the skill and patience of the dry stone wallers and the energy of people from all walks of life who gave up their weekends to dig, barrow, clear, build and plant. Children looked on in envy as tons of sticky mud was shovelled from 'the pond' to reveal, in true 'Time Team' fashion, a cobbled ford! The 19th century farm that Lilian Bond fondly remembers in her book, *Tyneham, A Lost Heritage,*

The granary 1943. The rickyard by the wall is now a wildflower meadow.

is gone. We cannot walk 'through the warm rows of stacks' in the rickyard or watch as 'manes and tails were plaited up with straw and coloured ribbons' in the stable but an echo of the past exists today. The wall bordering the rick-yard has been rebuilt complete with a traditional Purbeck barway instead of the usual wooden gate. The past lingers most in the dark damp Stable. Mouldering leather tack hangs limply from the walls and the worm eaten and crumbling partitions of the horse

Rusting collections of metal gather cobwebs on the window ledges in the stable.

stalls still stand. It is easy to imagine the warmth and bustle as horses were readied to take the wagons to town. In the centre of the farm is the History Barn, the focal point of the Tyneham Farm Project. This large airy space is ideal for displaying information. Racks of old tools and farm equipment line the stone walls and a grand blue and red wagon takes up much of the south bay. Dominating the scene and looking surprisingly comfortable in this unusual setting is a colourful stage.

In 2009 Lilian Bond's stage was recreated in the History Barn. Her childhood home is flooded with natural light as the sun streams down through the barn roof.

During the early years of the last century the barn was home to the Tyneham Theatre. Encouraged by their father, William Bond, the five children from 'the big house' put on productions here to raise money for a village hall. Lilian Bond recalls an audience of 160 coming from all over Dorset to see their plays and pantomimes. The last production was just before the outbreak of the 1914 war. Almost 100 years later in September 2009 the Purbeck Village Quire celebrated harvest on the recreated stage. Tyneham Theatre lives again! Lilian would have approved.

Any requests? Visitors are encouraged to perform on the stage in the barn.

Outside the barn, tucked under the shelter of its high south wall is the garden. Bathed in sun for most of the day and surrounded by walls, hedges and flowers this must be the warmest and most peaceful corner of the village. Rest a while here with only the butterflies, bees and hoverflies for company. The archway that leads into the garden is built through the back wall of the old cow stalls. All of the outbuildings that once bordered the cow yard have been lost. These narrow sheds enclosed the farmstead and housed the farm animals during the cold winter months. A high fence now encloses the farm, protecting hundreds of newly planted young trees and shrubs from the hungry mouths of Sika deer.

Farmhouse and Dairy. A mixture of horses, sheep, pigs and chickens roam free. The milking parlour X, now the public toilets, is the only surviving building.

"Is it an art installation?" The 'Scrappy Wall' is built on the footprint of the cow stalls, a jumble of rusting farm and military equipment, stone, bricks, pipes, ...

Tyneham Farm is not a restoration project but care is taken to preserve what remains. Buildings are kept weatherproof by the Army's main contractors, missing tiles replaced and failed timbers renewed. An air of carefully managed decay gives visitors a real sense of stepping back in time. The project is run by a local designer working for the Army's Range Liaison Officer who is based at nearby Lulworth Camp. Most of the outside work is done by voluntary groups. The Dorset Countryside Volunteers visit the farm about three times a year and have been responsible for much of the work in the 'pond yard'. The original course of the stream was restored on their first visit in 2009. Later tasks included building a footbridge and replacing patches of missing cobbles - in the pouring rain. Hard work but great fun! Annual maintenance continues. It is still a work in progress...

2013. On a warm August weekend volunteers clear accumulated silt from the cobbled ford. During the winter a stream flows through the gap in the wall.

The Army in Purbeck
Lynda Price, 2014

There has been a military presence in Purbeck since the reign of George III. In 1794 we were at war with France and the Dorset coast was vulnerable to attack. Local landowner Thomas Weld raised his own troop of men from his estate at Lulworth; any local man rich enough to provide his own horse, sword and pistol could become a soldier in the new Dorsetshire Volunteer Rangers. The threat from across the channel disappeared in 1815 after Waterloo but trouble was brewing locally.

Troops were drafted in to help the Coastguard catch the increasingly bold smugglers who were landing their contraband in remote bays such as Arish Mell and Worbarrow. By 1860 the young Queen Victoria had renamed the volunteers The Queen's Own Regiment of Yeoman Cavalry. Their annual tented camps on the coastal fields of the Weld Estate created much excitement amongst the locals. But the days of the bright dashing cavalry were almost over. The static entrenched fighting of WW1 saw the need for something to break the deadlock and in 1916 the tank was born. It was destined to change warfare, and Dorset, for ever. The newly formed Tank Corps at Bovington and the Gunnery School at Lulworth were established before the Great War ended in November 1918. Dorset had already become 'The Home of the Tank'.

The early tanks, limited to a range of 300 yards, were fired against the north slope of Bindon Hill, near Lulworth Camp. By 1938 its big,

1914 The last tented camp. Lord Kitchener's Army at Lulworth.
He was unimpressed with tanks, referring to them as 'pretty mechanical toys'.

Challenger 2 Main Battle Tank.
The only tank in use by the British Army.

powerful successors needed more space to practise live firing. Another war in Europe was inevitable, the situation was urgent. Coastal land to the east of Bindon was leased from the Weld Estate. The range boundary now extended past the tiny cove of Arish Mell to Flower's Barrow on the Chalk ridge above the Tyneham valley. **In 1943** as thousands of allied troops and armoured vehicles gathered in Britain to prepare for the invasion of Europe, Churchill's War Cabinet ordered the evacuation of Tyneham and the heathland north of the village. The south coast became an armed camp. Eleven million acres of land, much of it farmland, became airfields, camps, munitions dumps and training grounds. By the spring of 1944 the Tyneham valley had become part of the wartime 'Dorset Coast Battle Area', a training ground for American and British tank crews based at Lulworth and Bovington. Most of the Americans who trained at Tyneham were destined to leave Weymouth and Portland for 'Omaha Beach', the 'bloodiest' of the five Allied landing sites. Two and a half thousand lost their lives there on 6th June 1944 - D-Day.

Allied victory in 1945 did not bring the expected return home for villagers, farmers and smallholders evacuated during the winter of 1943. In 1948, with the Cold War looming, the land was compulsorily purchased by the Government from the landowners. Ralph Bond lost his ancestral estate and Tyneham became a permanent part of the Lulworth Army Ranges. **Since WW2** our troops have been sent to war zones all over the world. The ranges provide a vital training ground and are used by the military during the working week. All army personnel involved in the use of armoured fighting vehicles (AFV) are trained at Lulworth and Bovington. During the working week the ranges are used by the military. As soon as firing finishes, a team of wardens patrol the footpaths that are open to the public and check the beach and village. On Saturday morning the gates are unlocked and

Scimitar, a fast armoured reconnaissance vehicle which looks like a small tank.

the ranges become one of Dorset's most popular tourist attractions.

Tyneham Village is the focal point of the ranges. Most visitors are aware of its dramatic past but see little evidence of its present role as a training area for our forces. One of the few signs of military activity are the large, numbered wooden boards visible from the footpaths and roads. These boards are not 'targets' but Arc Markers which define the boundaries of different practice areas. The actual targets are half buried in the ground and electronically controlled, popping up when the range is in use.

Tyneham Range is one of several ranges that make up the twenty five square miles of The Lulworth Army Ranges. Modern weapons need large areas of empty land before they can safely fire. Each weapon and Range has its own safety zone known as a 'template'. A machine gun template is about two miles long, but when large artillery guns are firing on the Heath Range the template is huge, covering Tyneham and extending twelve miles out to sea, where Safety Boats patrol the danger area.

In 1916 the volunteers of the Yeomanry Cavalry charged into battle on horse-back with sabres drawn. Today, their Territorial Army successors in the Dorset Yeomanry train on one of the best equipped tanks in the world. The safety of troops is paramount. A Challenger 2 costs over four million pounds. Its crew are protected by highly specialised multi-layered armour and it can destroy an enemy tank from a distance of over two miles. In recent conflicts multi-functional armoured vehicles such as Scimitar and Warrior have proved their worth.

The British Army needs to adapt in the ever changing face of conflict. In 2012 the MoD announced its plan for the future structure of our armed forces. **Army 2020** sent shock waves through the establishment. The regular Army would be cut by 20,000 and all 16,000 troops based in Germany would return to Britain. The future will see more reliance on the volunteer troops of the Territorial Army. 15,000 more men and women need to be recruited and trained to meet the quota of 30,000. There will be more investment in smaller, more versatile armoured fighting vehicles. The Tank Corps will become a victim of this change of emphasis. With regiments merging, soldiers retraining and the potential of 15,000 raw recruits in the Territorial Army, the Lulworth Army Ranges will remain an important training facility for many years to come.

The Ministry of Defence is one of the largest landowners in Britain. The Lulworth Army Ranges are one of the sixteen major training areas held solely for training our armed forces. The range covers about twenty five square miles. Its coastline runs from Kimmeridge Bay to Lulworth Cove, a total of six and a half miles.